JOURNEY TO THE "Y" IN YOU

DENE E. GAINEY

Journey to the "Y" in You:
Your Guide to Understanding Why it Had to Happen
by Dene Gainey
Published by EduMatch®
PO Box 150324, Alexandria, VA 22315
www.edumatch.org

© 2018 Dene Gainey

All rights reserved. No portion of this book may be reproduced in any form without permission from the publisher, except as permitted by U.S. copyright law. For permissions contact sarah@edumatch.org.

Cover by Omichele Gainey

ISBN-13: 978-1-970133-15-8

In Dedication

To a man of wisdom and strength, until his transition from this life to the next, who knew more than I did, saw further than I did, and guided me to where I am today.

To a man that loved and valued education so much that he achieved his doctoral degree at the ripe age of 71.

To a man that I called "Daddy" who is now in heaven.

Thank you for taking the time to bring out the best in me. I dedicate this inaugural book to you, knowing you'd be proud and probably be wearing a similar grin on your face, like the day of my US Air Force graduation.

Dr. Daniel E. Gainey
Doctor of Theology
1938-2013

To my mother, Margaret Jones, thank you for continuing to be such a great support in all that I undertake.

Expressions of Gratitude

To my Aunt Mary, who went through the initial script of this book with a fine-tooth comb and straightened out every crooked path, thank you.

To the 12 years' worth of students I have taught and the relationships that have been cultivated through time, thank you.

To all the educators who continue to work in the trenches, thank you.

Preface

I'd like to first say thank you for picking up a copy of this inaugural book. You may be wondering the context in which this book was written. Let me assure you that it will likely make you think, reflect, question, and consider new ideas or perspectives. Most of all, I hope it causes you to act, to be. I hope that somehow you are encouraged through the anecdotes you will read in these pages to keep pushing to be the best (and only) version of you.

I quickly realized that our unique traits are essential to our individuality and is necessary because it creates an opportunity for you to see the good in others, as well as to be able to offer unique experiences and understanding to those unlike yourself. In this tangled web we weave called life, we all have stories that should be told. Imagine the impact you would make if you told your story. Consider that one individual, who decides to keep persevering because your story gave them the courage to do so. Consider that group of teachers just entering the field of education, who will encounter challenges you may be able to curb or assist with because of your unique experiences.

This book started as a series of separate writing pieces that were eventually woven together to form a fabric called *The Y in You*. The

PREFACE

question is, "What's the "why" in you?" Why do you? Why would you? Why should you?

I hope that through the pages in this book, you will gain the confidence to be you, and understand the power in what being you can produce. From philosophy to personal experiences, from existential considerations to the very nature of the human experience, I encourage you to think about who might be waiting on you to be you.

Foreword

It was May of 1999. There I was, sitting in Pre-Calculus class at Saint Joseph's Collegiate Institute in Buffalo, New York. It was my last day of high school. The clock was about to strike 2:30 PM - dismissal time. Ready with my Kodak Fun Saver 35mm disposable camera, I just had to capture a picture of the clock at this exact moment. I had taken some photos throughout the day with friends, so I could save some memories of what were, at the time, the best four years of my life. Little did I know that the best years were still ahead of me. Oh, the advice I could give to my younger self!

Anyway, my intention in taking a picture of the clock right at 2:30 PM was to capture the moment I would be done with math class for good! It didn't come easy. I had to work very hard for the grades I earned. I didn't cut the Advanced Placement class for Calculus. I remember working so hard at that Pre-Calculus class and taking the photo of the clock would symbolize the sense of relief that it was over. My Journey to the "Y" in You (Me) started well before this moment. I didn't realize it at the time, but I was already heading down a certain path, a path shaped by others in my life in both big and small ways.

2:30 PM struck. I got the picture.

FOREWORD

One of my goals was to become an optometrist. My mother was a K-12 vision teacher for the visually impaired in an area school district. My father operated a wholesale optical lab in Buffalo, NY. (Ironically, they met on a "blind" date. True story.)

My father started the business with a handful of customers in the basement of our house in 1981 when I was just one year old. Talk about scary...a newborn at home and entering into the unknown of starting your own business. I had it all planned out to follow in those footsteps in that career field.

I loved school, loved learning and loved my education journey to this point. I visited colleges based on their science programs with the goal of going to graduate school for optometry. Kind of ironic that I didn't quite have the vision to look ahead at how my journey would take shape.

Integrated into my college visits and selection were schools with a good ice hockey program. Another one of my goals was to play NCAA ice hockey at the collegiate level, since I played competitively at a high level through my youth. Here were a few subtle ways my journey started to take shape.

My passion and calling were beginning to collide without me fully realizing it. Dene references this in his book when he also talks of the passion and the call colliding. My mother's parents were a teacher and administrator, so teaching was in our family lineage. My hockey coaches were some of my best teachers, for the sport of hockey and for life. I didn't make the college selection process easy on myself by applying to 11 schools and visiting even more. I always followed my heart and it always had a way of working out. It was as though these two forces set to intersect.

I ended up at SUNY Geneseo, a small college just outside of

FOREWORD

Rochester, NY, playing hockey for the Ice Knights. The team was made up of mainly business majors. I was one of the few education majors (there were three of us on a team of 25 hockey players).

Wait, education major? That biology major ended up realizing that becoming an optometrist was not the journey I was meant to be on. It was not my "Y." I changed my degree track to mathematics with a secondary education concentration. I'll say the rest is history, since I really want you to get into the story Dene Gainey has set before you, rather than sharing much more of mine.

The truth is, there is so much more to the story. In fact, we all have a unique journey, a unique story. The diversity in these stories is what makes being a part of this world so special. You will learn from this book that diversity and community is something that should be honored and celebrated.

Going back to that last math class of high school waiting to take the picture...I feel terrible as I write this, but I cannot remember my math teacher's name. I am going to have to go back to the yearbook to look it up. It could be partially old age contributing to this forgetfulness.

The reality is that this teacher just taught math. He sure taught me math well enough that I applied it beyond high school, and eventually earned a mathematics degree in college. The thing is, he didn't create the impact where it was impossible to forget his name. He didn't "reach" me. He didn't C.L.I.M.B.E.

The ironic thing about taking the picture of the clock as I was leaving math class to celebrate not having another math class is that I became a math teacher. Yep, I spent 10 years spending most of my days in a math classroom as my career. When a former student sees me and says, "Hi Mr. Drezek," even several years later, I know I made enough of an impact where a relationship was formed, and s/he remembered my name. They say relationships are the key to just about everything and I would have to agree!

FOREWORD

❦

This is just a snapshot of my journey, which continues to evolve. I've evolved from math teacher to district technology integration specialist as a teacher on special assignment. I've grown from being rated a 1 out of 20 by New York State Education Department (a score based on student growth formulas) to being named as New York State Computers and Technology in Education (NYSCATE, a branch of ISTE) Teacher of the Year.

This teaching thing will not be easy. It can't be easy. It shouldn't be easy. This teaching thing, however, could be worth it. It should be worth it. It will be worth it!

Along the way we'll feel like we are experiencing more losses than wins. There will be others that will try to dim your light. Surround yourself with those like Dene Gainey, who will brighten your path and help you shine brighter.

My journey involves realizing that we are never "finished" and always working towards something. Outside of the classroom, my journey has evolved from son, to husband, to father. The reality is that I ended up in education for many of the same reasons as Dene, yet also for many different reasons. The amazing thing is that on this journey, our paths crossed. We are so connected on this planet...so much more than we can ever truly understand.

❦

I am writing this foreword today because of our journeys to our Y. The journeys are uniquely ours, but also shared. This is the journey to the U in us. We are so much better together.

The cover of this book states, "Why you? Why not you?" Dene asks the ultimate question. Why NOT you? Why not us? Why not now? I am so glad you are picking up this book and making Dene's journey part of yours. People like Dene are making a true impact on students within their classroom, and through their writing, they are reaching and influencing students and people both near and far. I am

FOREWORD

so grateful that Dene has created this book, this guide to understanding just why "it" had to happen.

Everyone is searching for his or her "Y." Some discover it earlier in life, some later, some possibly in the moments of reading this book, and some always remain in discovery mode. In life, I cannot think of anything much more important than discovering our "Y." The Journey to the "Y" in YOU is just that, a journey. It's your "Y." It's your "why."

Dene Gainey takes you along for the ride on his journey to becoming the man he is today. This is a man who I am proud to call a friend...one I can lean on for advice and support: advice that isn't sugar coated in any way, and support that is ongoing. Dene is as authentic and genuine as they come.

Reading his book will not lay out answers for you. It will however steer you down a path towards your answers, your "Y." The road there lies in the inner reflection, the relation to the story, the similarities and the differences. There is so much power in this story and in these questions.

There is a good chance reading this book will make you tear up, with some sadness, but far more joy. Everyone has a story to tell and there is so much we can learn by taking the time to hear someone else's. I hope you enjoy Dene's story and the journey to his "Y" as much as I did. I hope we can all become a little more like Dene, while also becoming the best version of ourselves. Our students can only benefit from this and the world might just become a better place along the way.

Dene is a true harmonizer in the field of education. He can bring a room full of people together at an edcamp. He can bring an auditorium of people to their feet while singing at an ISTE Karaoke event. He can bring hundreds of educators together over #FLedchat on Twitter. Dene is a true changemaker. Dene is the teacher you wish your own child had each school year to put your mind at ease.

This is his call to you....to bring you together over a few chapters with the intention of helping you discover your "Y" and why it had to happen and is happening at this very moment. After reading this book, I am also confident you will connect and gravitate toward those

FOREWORD

teachers in your school, and in your professional networks who are like Dene. Enjoy and embrace what is to come on your journey ahead. Get ready to "C.L.I.M.B.E."

Michael Drezek
District Technology Integration Specialist, Lake Shore Central Schools

When "They" Don't Know Your Name

Everybody has a name, right? It is by name that we are identified when we line the delivery room walls for parents and viewers to see all the newborn babies. So, we are known by our name, and who or what we become is linked to that name. While my role is an educator, I am also a singer, writer, actor, and mentor. Any perspectives shared in this text might be from the perspective of an educator, but truly, anyone could fit this bill.

As we grow and mature, we understand desires, dreams, and goals. I believe it is safe to assume that everyone has dreams, goals, and aspirations about where they'd like to be at some juncture in their lives. More specifically, I believe that there is an innate passion and desire to act, to do, to be, to accomplish, and to leave some sort of legacy here on this planet we call Earth. We were born unaware of what we would face in life, the challenges that would creep up on us, or the trials and tribulations that would plague our existence. Perhaps as kids, we could not fully understand the greatness that lies within us. But with age and maturity, here we are.

Much of my life has included analysis, as well as strong critique of situations and circumstances that I have had to deal with. I am naturally an analytical person, always trying to understand the why of everything, and to draw conclusions regarding the nature of occurrences or experiences. Perhaps this is not the greatest trait to have, but through the analysis of life, I have concluded that the thing that drives you and compels you to do what you do *cannot be halted*, even when "they" don't know your name.

I started my teaching career in January of 2004 after an eventful four years of college at the University of Central Florida in Orlando. Interestingly, I knew since I was 9 years old that my path would lead me to the classroom. My first-grade teacher, Mrs. Enid K. Sweeting, is to be commended for her inspiration, love, and concern for me, even at that age. It was also thanks to her that I was able to write with neater handwriting than most of my peers - a skill which I have carried over to the present day.

It was because of her that I went back every year to help with her classroom officially starting in middle school, but also as an elementary student when I left the first grade, all the way up until my graduation from high school.

My point is that your beliefs and your actions, what you do and how you do it, are inextricably linked to **WHO** you are. I hope that this book will help you to develop confidence in yourself. Further, you may never truly have your name in lights, and though "they" may not remember your name, as the cliché goes, your actions speak louder.

Reflection Questions

- Reflect on an experience you've had, or something you've done, for which you were not given credit. How did it shape you?
- Identify three traits that describe your character. How did these traits become part of you?

The C.L.I.M.B.E. Philosophy

As a tree "climbs" and produces fruit, so does this philosophy.

You might be wondering, what is the C.L.I.M.B.E. philosophy, and how does it pertain to education?

I firmly believe that there is a need for role models, mentors, and individuals to make a difference in their area of influence. How then, does this philosophy apply? This is an idea that I have been developing for some time. Students must have insight, wisdom, and guidance for both the future of society and their own well-being. It is important that the knowledge and experience that one has is shared with others; otherwise, it leaves the earth with that individual.

I am a lifelong learner.

C (Cultivate)

It is important to cultivate the quality of "knowledge seeker" within students, being free and driven to explore passions and creativity in life. They need an environment where there are no limits to the learning that can occur; where they are free to be who they are and who they want to be.

The benefit of cultivating an environment conducive to learning is that it has a lasting impact on our students. On a random day, one student conveyed that he couldn't wait to get to my classroom because, "It is like an adventure, I never know what is going to happen until I get there." I was completely humbled.

This student is now a middle schooler but the impact this comment had on me, other than a smile, was that it inspired me to continue to be spontaneous and to loosely frame the day as a day of exploration. I make lesson plans; however, things don't always go as planned.

The student in question was very involved, motivated, and assumed leadership in many ways within the classroom. He kept me on my toes, too. If I ever made an error or mistake, he didn't have a problem correcting me. I loved that. Why not cultivate an environment where your students can help you just as much as you help them, if not more? That's what I call a student-driven classroom.

When an environment is cultivated for learning (and growing), you remove the limits. Learning can happen in ways you didn't realize. In addition, students are excited to enter, they are engaged, and they go beyond your expectations.

L (Lead)

With any great organization, there must be solid leaders. Such leaders must be developed. Students need to understand what it means to lead and be granted opportunities to do so, even in the developmental years. Leaders can take shape throughout the classroom, particularly when students are involved in decision-making and planning the learning in some way.

Naturally we (educators) serve as leaders in our classrooms, and hopefully we are working to also develop students as leaders. There are two anecdotes that cannot go without mention. The first of two includes a student who most teachers might have defined as a "handful." What a transformation that took place when he was given some responsibility!

The student required a fair amount of redirection early on, but one day he'd asked to facilitate an aspect of our class. This was an English Language Arts class and everything in it, diversified at best, was used to develop literacy - including discussions about literature, thoughts, and quotes. I allowed the student to take over the discussions, and the transformation began. He was still the same individual who walked in my room physically, but he developed leadership whereby he was able to think deeply, engage others, and on some days blew me away with his thought process. When provided the space and opportunity, students will take that leadership capacity and run with it. I was in awe. There were days I would wonder - *what if I had not given him the chance?* It would have clearly been a missed opportunity for both of us.

Like the previously mentioned student, another in each class period stepped up to the plate and demonstrated initiative. The discussions were rich, meaningful, and focused. The best part is that others participated and provided their perspectives and viewpoints. What diversity of opinion! Sharing viewpoints helped all students to grow from being able to listen to others. If they didn't agree, then it was an opportunity to teach students how to disagree respectfully. These three students became leaders right before my eyes.

THE SECOND OF the anecdotes is another student who demonstrated initiative, and now faithfully reviews what I call the "reading daily warm-up." Through his decision to take on this leadership role, he has matured so much intellectually and leads the review as if it were a teacher standing there. Clearly he is still a student, but I publicly praise his leadership and reinforce his efforts. Again, if you allow a student the space and opportunity to act, s/he will. In fact, I will go as far as to say that s/he will never be the same because of it.

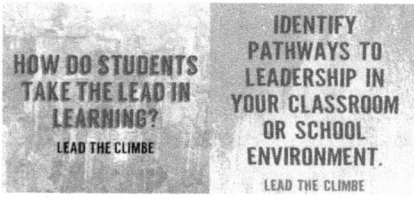

I (Inspire)

As a teacher, I take great pride in this aspect of the philosophy. You never know who you might be teaching or what result that teaching will produce. Therefore, there is no such thing as "small inspiration." Create a spark, add a log to a fire, and allow students the opportunity to feel around, poke around, and explore.

I am honored to have had a variety of experiences: the arts (acting and singing), writing, the military, and some travel. These components of my life come with me into the classroom. More specifically, they help me to *reach* my students.

Perhaps the real reason why I like doing these things is because they broaden my reach. I can relate to the students who sing or have the desire to; I understand the actors and actresses and the related experiences; and yet I have learned discipline and can offer stories to my students that inspire them to be "more."

One such experience was a student who did not have confidence in herself but possessed a great love for the arts. My proclivity and passion for the arts would often show itself when I would break into random songs in the middle of class. Whether connected to a concept being taught or not, the songs would reach my students along with the words of encouragement I often provided.

This might be a good example of when lesson plans didn't go "as planned." The next thing you know, the idea of a non-traditional genius hour came to mind and the student was ready to showcase her talent. She was extremely nervous, but she was ready. She blew the class away with the power and confidence in her voice, and her versatility in working the scale with high and low notes. Since then, she has (even though nervously) participated multiple times and has become surer of a direction in life she wants to pursue. She needed to have an example, which inspired her to try, which led to her success. What if we really made the most of inspirational moments? The results just may be revolutionary.

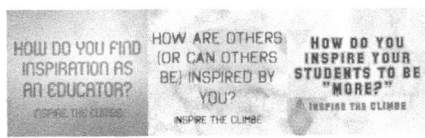

M (Motivate)

This speaks for itself. I have always believed that motivation is 75% of my job. If I can motivate students, then everything else is easy. Motivation is the desire of an individual to act, to think, or to achieve something. Research suggests that student achievement is a direct result of motivation.[1] What is taught should contain an element of motivation, which might include authenticity and relevance.

There are countless examples of stories here. I firmly believe that if you tell someone something that they don't believe long enough, eventually they begin to believe it.

This might be the best example of my thoughts on motivation. How do you motivate another individual to believe or to act? I recall a specific example of a student I taught in 2017. The student came in as very coy and quiet. I remember the very first day she walked into my room. She was very reserved, as if trying to take it all in. That didn't last long!

She became pretty vocal over time, gradually asking questions and participating in class discussions. It was as if she needed a spark to light the flame and since that time, the flame has grown bigger and bigger. She became an "all in" kind of student. Her mom had even commented to me on occasion, how motivated her daughter was, and how she didn't know what had happened to cause it. She also shared that she is always working on something relative to school and learning. It made my day to hear the parent's comments; it was as if every stride I had ever made was realized, and worth it.

Asking this student questions and answering the questions she had was of particular importance. It was engagement, interaction with the student, and genuine encouragement that she needed. Once those was established, growth immediately began. As a secondary consideration, it became very clear that the student was responding to a teacher who empowered her. It wasn't enough for me to deliver content knowledge, but she understood the value of seeking, searching, pondering, wondering, questioning, and even verifying her learning.

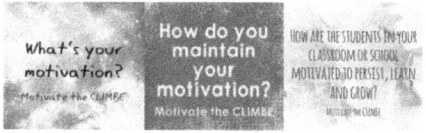

B (Build)

What does it mean to build? You might say, "to form, to construct, or to empower." I believe that through good habits, organizational skills, and opportunity, students can build their confidence and ability. There is no "little thing" I do in the classroom. It is all intentional, deliberate, and on purpose with their future in mind.

To build a house, you need a plan. Otherwise the house may not turn out as you intended. In addition, it will not stand without a proper foundation. When I consider who I am today, I am a product of the skills, habits, and development attained in the process of building me. A house may look amazing on the outside and lack the internal components that provide structure and stability. You may say that character is the form of internal stability of our foundation.

I believe in building student character above all. Again, what good is a house without internal structure? Thus, the outward expression of an individual is likely relative to the inward components. Those inward components allow us to develop the capacity to understand each other (empathy), to see reason, and to work together.

E (Enrich & Empower)

In my mind, to enrich means to stretch. A rubber band's potential can only be realized when it is stretched. I tell my students that they won't leave my class the same way that they came in. By the time they leave, they will believe things that they may not have believed in the beginning. I say to them, **"You will realize that the power to excel lies within you."**

Students thrive in an environment of empowerment where there is culture, where there is thrill, where there is opportunity to think outside of the box, and where their perspectives are valued, listened to, and given credence to. These provide motivation to continue to think outside of the box and remain active participants in the class.

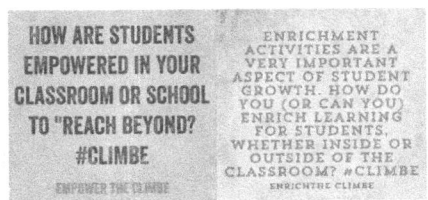

Reflection Questions

1. What is one thing you can do right now to help your students and/or colleagues to C.L.I.M.B.E?
2. What is your personal or professional philosophy when it comes to growth and development? What perspectives constitute your practice?

The Success Initiative

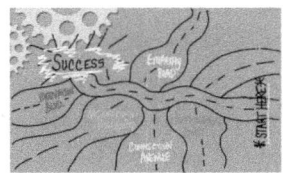

> "A successful man is one who can lay a firm foundation with the bricks that others have thrown at him."

David Brinkley was onto something when he coined this eloquent phrase, which makes me think about the following questions:

1. What is success?
2. What is the purpose of a foundation?
3. What are these bricks?

Is success a relative idea? Some may equate success to having lots of money in the bank, driving nice cars, living in a luxurious home, taking expensive vacations, or acquiring power and prestige.

Is this truly success? Does an individual have success when these items are achieved? What if you have some, but not all of these elements? Does having one make you successful, versus having all five? Is it safe to assume that if one does not have any of these great material things, that he or she is not successful? Perhaps it is important to reevaluate what success really means for ourselves as well as for the students that look up to us.

It is important to strive, reach, push, pull, grind, and do all that can be done. As educators, we help our students to prepare (or be prepared) for life; we help them to have a solid foundation on which they can continue to build, expand, and grow.

The house may never be finished. Ask the lifelong learners; they will tell you that learning is perpetual. If learning were a house, you might as well come over anytime for a visit because it will never be complete enough; there is always more to learn. A foundation then is the lowest part of a building, upon which the other parts rest.

What are these bricks, you say? In the literal sense, bricks are rectangular, 3-D objects, often used to line the walls of houses or other buildings. You might recall the childhood story of *The Three Little Pigs* and the differences between the houses they built of straw, sticks, and bricks. The wolf was no match for the house built with bricks because they were solid, heavy, and provided structure to the third pig's house.

What can be learned from this? Perhaps something quite profound, such that it may totally transform your perspective on the challenges in life.

Physical bricks solidify the house. Metaphorically speaking, bricks might include negativity or judgment. They may also be that constant struggle to be yourself. The fault-finding brick may hit you, as no one truly is perfect. The brick might be that expectation for you to know everything without ever learning or being taught.

It's very possible that the brick has a purpose. We've heard the saying many times, "what doesn't kill you makes you stronger." Some bricks are necessary, because while they may have been thrown to attack your credibility, worth, or integrity, these bricks can be added to the house.

So then, how does one use these "bricks" as a benefit?

Certainly, it requires a perspective shift. How you embrace these things in life is all based on perception. Our perception can either build us up or defeat us. What would happen if we viewed every challenge, obstacle, or hurdle as an opportunity to build, grow, and change? Maybe that's a lofty goal. However, consider how you win when you challenge yourself to see the bricks differently.

All things considered, we can't always avoid the bricks. But, we can make the bricks work FOR us. Therefore, we can see success differently. We can see success as winning, going through it rather than around it, knowing there might be something in the brick that really pushes us closer toward what success really is. It's not simply what you have, but what you do regardless of what you have.

Reflection Questions

1. How do you define success?
2. Reflect on an experience that you considered successful. What was the biggest obstacle?
3. Is success really success without challenges or obstacles? Why or why not?

We Have the Light

> *A good teacher is like a candle - it consumes itself to light the way for others.*
> ~ Mustafa Kemal Ataturk

I had to read this quote a few times because it was just that packed with depth. There are a few words that stand out to me here: candle, consumes, light, way, and others. Unpacking this quote serves as the foundation for this chapter. It is the very essence of being a teacher, an educator, a mentor, a guide.

Candle

When you think of a candle, the first thought is probably an item that when lit by a spark, provides heat and light to a place (perhaps a room) or a person. Candles come in many different shapes and sizes, as well as colors and fragrances. Right away, this aspect of a candle is comparative to the different types of people in the world.

One of the greatest "unifiers" in my mind is the idea that we are not all the same. As a candle has many different physical properties, they all provide heat and light. Metaphorically speaking, *heat* might be comfort or warmth; in a person, perhaps it is the nature of an individual that makes him or her relatable. *Light*, which we will talk more about later, creates a way to see what would not be seen without it. Considering these candle properties, it is no wonder a teacher is compared to a candle; students we interact with may lack actual heat and light, but metaphorically could also lack comfort, support, and guidance.

Consume

The term *consume* has many meanings. A definition we will use is to "engage fully" or "to enjoy avidly,"[1] as provided by Merriam Webster.

There is a huge difference between collecting a paycheck as a teacher in a classroom and doing all you can and being all that you can, while you can. What greater reward is there than the knowledge that you have worked tirelessly to help shape "today?" If I am not going to give something 100% of me while I am doing it, then I'd rather not do it.

There is much to be said about dedication and passion. The candle burns once lit, and as it burns, it consumes itself. With every new opportunity to disseminate knowledge or facilitate learning, we put our all into it; we fully embrace teaching and learning, as the reward is immense. Will it be monetary? You never know, but money is of no value when compared to knowing you have lit someone else's path.

The Light

Light is necessary to see your way through dark situations, both literally and figuratively. When you walk into a dark room, it is necessary to flip the switch in most cases to map the path in which you will travel and arrive at the destination without incident. When there is no light, we may stumble, become injured, collide with others or things, and essentially lose focus of the initial goal. We need the light because it illuminates the path and clarifies the way in which we are to reach our destination(s). Students, particularly in their developmental years, need to know where to go and they need guidance along the way. There may be a myriad of reasons why the light isn't always there. If it does happen to be there for them, it is not always on. Therefore, as educators we must be a light, or **the** light.

The Way

When you think about the word "way," you might envision a sidewalk, a street, a highway, or maybe even a path in the water or sky. Have you ever been in the car and realized that you were going the wrong way?

We, the educators of our students, must show them the way — the **right** way, to keep them from going the wrong way. The wrong way could lead to devastation and turmoil. In their worlds, we may be the only positive forces. Some might not want to leave our classrooms or schools because they can see and feel that someone cares about their *way*.

Another perspective would be the "way" in which students act, work, or present themselves. We do not want our students to act in a "way" that is inappropriate; therefore, we work hard to build their character so that they will take these practices with them as they matriculate through their educational paths and beyond.

Others

When you consider others, you are practicing selflessness. I am in no way saying that you should not consider yourself. You must take care of you because if you don't, it is possible that no one will. However, the selfless teacher knows that students have needs, and regards his or her actions for the purpose and benefit of his or her students. The students are the most important stakeholders in our schools because students benefit from all that we do. When our focus is on the students, or on *others*, we are driven to see that the students excel. When we focus on others, we succeed when they succeed.

Reflection Questions

1. Consider a time when you were a light to someone else. Was it intentional or unintentional? What was the story, and how did the experience impact you?
2. What is your perspective on guiding students? How do you show them the way?

Turn the Page

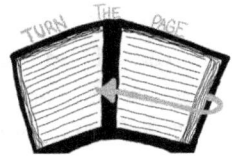

Life is a collection of experiences. The experiences that make up life, both good and bad, are necessary to mold, shape, develop, and stabilize us in ever-changing times. Many people say that the only consistent thing in life is change. Tragedy is never a welcomed event, but one thing is certain: it is in the challenges of life that we become stronger, better equipped, and more vigilant. As educators, I believe that we have a great task on our hands.

Being a doctoral student, one thing I have become very familiar with is turning the page because of the great amount of reading that is necessary to learn and grow. Life could be compared to a book. We might say that the pages of the book reflect days in our lives, or perhaps the experiences that shape us continually. Sometimes it is a difficult thing to turn the page. It takes strength. It takes courage. It takes forward thinking. It takes a certain drive to persist amidst the vicissitude of recent days. Our hearts hurt because we are human beings, full of emotion, trying to piece things together to see the complete picture.

Does it all make sense to me? Certainly, I do not have all the answers, but one thing I do know — it is important that we turn the page. Let's not stay there. I think that times like these remind me as an educator, of several things:

1. to be better.
2. to be genuine.
3. to be an example.
4. to be a light.

One of the lessons I use in the classroom daily challenges my students to be better. Though there is nothing wrong with being average, I challenge them to not settle for average or the status quo. I ask, "What stands out about you?" or "What will people notice when they look at you?"

It's easy to blend in with the crowd, but why not take that extra step and be authentic? For a student, that might mean instead of waiting for me to ask certain questions, he or she seeks that knowledge using available resources. I think the same applies to me as the educator. Once I stop learning, I am limited in the knowledge I can pass on to my students. Thus, I am always reading or involving myself in some way to continue in my own development to be better.

"Genuine" means that I really care when I say that I do. Or perhaps, I demonstrate what I say. I know we have all experienced a letdown or two in life (perhaps even more than that). However, imagine how you would feel if you knew, by word and deed, that the person acting on your behalf was genuine. Would you invest more, trust more, engage more, if you knew that the individual truly cares about you? Educators just might be the bridge that takes a student from one side of the water to the other. An educator might be the reason that a student decides to care more about what they do and how they do it. An educator might be the reason why gaps are filled, and support is felt by both students and their families alike.

I am all for setting a positive example, a visual representation of the possibilities. As a visual model, we provide the hope that students can learn, grow, and develop to do whatever they choose. There is no limit to the learning that can occur when we are the example. Does that mean that every educator needs to hold advanced degrees? In my opinion, not necessarily. However, it does mean that teachers can demonstrate how to seize opportunities and show students that things can be attained.

I am grateful for the creative and artistic talents that I have, as well as my time as a uniformed service member of the US Air Force. These strong skills come into the classroom with me every day. In addition, the idea that I am a doctoral student provides an example to students that you can do anything, and that our greatest limits are ourselves.

What is light? Light is the absence of darkness. Light and darkness cannot exist in the same place. Darkness may be described as any place where there is no hope, concern, care, or love. It may just mean that someone needs another to care.

As educators, I believe that we are the catalysts for change. I believe that we can bring light into dark places. Considering recent events and things that happen in all our lives, an immense opportunity lies before us. We can be the reason that our students pursue the proper path with persistence. We can be the motivation for why students keep trying when things may not go as planned. We, the educators, can be lights on paths that are dimly lit or dark. Potentially, we can be the reason why someone turns the page.

Reflection Questions

1. What talents, skills, or experiences do you have that could encourage others/your students (if you are an educator)?
2. How would you approach others (your students) if you knew that the power of impact was guaranteed?
3. Why is perseverance so important? How would you (or do you) teach tenacity to students?

When the Call and the Passion Collide

Some may say that being an educator is a profession of choice. Others might say that one becomes a teacher because his or her parents or grandparents were teachers. I propose that neither of the two is accurate enough to describe the integral role that educators play in the lives of everyone.

There were behaviors I was born with, like crying for example. On the other hand, many things were only grasped because someone taught me. Whether the individual doing the teaching had an official title or not, he or she was instrumental in guiding me along to learn the concept, principle, or idea. We might say that the teacher(s) decided to act because there was something that I needed to learn and that they were able to teach me. Naturally, I learned from them.

As a kid, I grew up in a very strict household, where my parents expected me to do as I was instructed, and I was responsible for handling my schoolwork. I had the great privilege of connecting with my first-grade teacher, who I still admire and respect today. She had a way about her, demonstrating care and concern, yet holding me accountable for my actions. What's more is that she had such a great personality, and I found much of my interaction with her to be fun and enjoyable. It was her tender-yet-strict-and-caring nature that inspired me. It inspired me so much that I would go back to her classroom every day while I was a student at Hallandale Elementary School to serve as a student helper.

Throughout middle school and high school, I would continue to go back and visit, to offer my help in the classroom. I graduated from high school with the second highest amount of community service hours because of my *passion* for doing what she did. This passion might be a result of the call I felt, like her, to be part of the educator community. So yes, I knew somewhere deep down since I was a first grader that I would teach in a classroom. You might say, "that's not possible," or, "that's crazy…you were too young to know what you wanted to do." Perhaps the call to teach was always there and my first-grade teacher cultivated it or watered the seed such that I can walk in that role today. I am an educator today because of her.

What is a *call*? A call is a cry made as a summons or to attract someone's attention.[1] It can also be defined as an appeal or demand for something to happen or be done. It is a powerful force of attraction. The educator feels a strong pull to interact with students and to see them learn and grow. The educator answers that *call* by following the path to earning the necessary credentials, and ultimately walking into the classroom ready to meet the needs of students he or she will teach.

What does the call sound like? I propose that there is no sound, but rather there is an inward longing to act, to pass on knowledge, to allow for knowledge creation, to cultivate minds, to empower, to build, to enrich.

What is *passion*? Passion also has multiple definitions: an intense desire or enthusiasm for something, a strong and barely uncontrollable emotion, a state or outburst of strong emotion.[2] I place great value on deciding to give something my all. Why do anything halfway? If you go into a forest halfway, you might as well go all the way, because you'll have to backtrack that half to get out of the forest.

Being passionate is not only noticeable, but it is contagious. If you are passionate about what you do, consider the passion "electric" so that you can't even be near someone else without transference of an electric charge. What would happen if passion became electrically transferred because you decided that you were going in 100%? How would this new passionate attitude transform the mindsets and wills to learn of those you work with? How challenged would others feel to be better based on your decision to be better? The call and the passion can collide into an explosion of robust proportions.

What happens when the call collides with an individual's passion? There is a huge difference between just being "present" and being "passionate."

The *passionate* are excited and motivated to embrace challenges, be the counselors, nurses if needed, and to get down in the trenches with the students. The *passionate* understand the value of learning so much that they will continue to learn and grow to become better at their job. The *passionate* do not allow complacency to set in because they know that students are the ultimate recipients of all the hard work put into education. The *passionate* engage and interact with other educators to develop and collaborate through professional learning networks. The *passionate* develop their craft or skill through professional development avenues such as conferences, workshops, and social media designed to learn.

In May of 2016, I began to learn about various opportunities of which I was not previously aware. I happened to jump on Twitter to create an account, in hopes of connecting with other educators.

When you think about an outlet used to transfer power through a cord, educators are extension cords who are plugged into the source, whether directly or as an extension of someone else's cord. The power of connection is just that, power! We have the power to change the world when we answer the call and are passionately in pursuit of continued development.

Reflection Questions

1. What are you being "called" to do?
2. What is the thing that you feel most strongly about (passion)?
3. How does passion transform a mindset or a will to do?

Going the Extra Mile

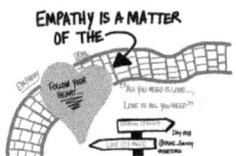

I understand that students today experience so much pressure to succeed and do well, but often lack the proper support systems with which to manage the challenges that they face from day to day. What does that look like?

It could be the girl or boy who has both parents at home, but still needs extra support. It might be that teenage kid that is the product of a single-parent home, and the parent is doing all that they can to support him/her. It might be a child who does not have a very good relationship with his or her parents and is looking for a model or a mentor. It may be that child who likes what s/he sees and seeks to emulate you, but lacks the steps or knowledge necessary to do so. It might be the child who has both parents in the picture but living in two different homes. Lastly, it could be that well-supported child with both parents providing aid to him or her, pushing them to do their very best, but the child still looks to you to be their guide. Whichever the experience, it is never a bad thing for an educator to go the extra mile.

Have you heard the phrase, "to whom much is given, much will be required?[1]" It is one thing to quote this, but it is another thing altogether to see this idea unfold. The benefits are great, but our job is about so much more than that. Teachers are not always appreciated for the hard work they do. It is a profession full of challenges from year to year, or even from day to day. However, educators are compelled not only to answer the call to teach and facilitate learning, but to go back every day with a renewed passion for bringing hope, light, strength, and empowerment to the students he or she teaches.

As teachers, our students are the *why* of what we do. If the educator embraces the mentality of going the extra mile, then the students are better for it. In fact, you're in a better position to encourage students to reach higher and dig deeper, as you are the model for it. There are no limits except for the ones set forth in the mind of the child, which could be because of what he or she does or does not experience. What if we created experiences for children to reach and aim? What if we cultivated an environment where students were intrinsically inspired to do more? What if taking this step in even one classroom is the spark to the flame to transforming education, as we know it?

What does it mean to "go the extra mile?" The idiomatic phrase could encompass a variety of different tools, strategies, tricks, or tactics demonstrated by the educator to bridge gaps, support students in their learning, bring hope or light to a challenging situation or simply put a smile on a student's face.

Last school year, I had a student, who we shall call Brooke. She came to me with challenges in the Language Arts content area, and I immediately began to work with her, to help her grow to a level that was consistent with grade level expectations. Things were progressing nicely; but as the year went on, I began to learn of other challenges faced by Brooke that may have placed limits on her learning. I decided to get involved and act as another support system for Brooke, who I hoped would come to me whenever she needed help, and to make some good of a difficult situation.

Because of the extra time spent with this student, the demonstration of care and concern and the establishment of an unofficial mentoring relationship with Brooke, there was a complete turnaround. Not only was there an increased motivation on Brooke's part, but she academically began to excel, and while not completely out of the woods, was making great strides to get there. I found myself attending extracurricular activities to support her, as well as devising ways to interact with her during the school day. This was a positive step, and it made a positive change in Brooke's life. The parent was thrilled with the change in Brooke's behavior due in part because I simply took time.

I love diversity and all that it brings to any situation. It is great to learn from others, and our experiences and viewpoints are all so varied and meaningful. That said, I have noticed that students tend to look for those they feel they can relate to at school. That may mean girls will cling to warm, inviting female teachers, or that minority students may look for minority teacher representation within the school. This is not division in any way, but simply their search for a model to pattern themselves after. The second scenario includes a student I will refer to as David, who I initially taught, but then returned to me in a different capacity for support.

David was dealing with the challenge of balancing life with a mom and dad who lived in separate homes. In addition, he was on a search to understand, or learn, who he really was. David had been having behavioral challenges at school because he was trying to fit in, balance home life, school life, and at the same time, face the quest to identify himself. I listened to him, allowed him to come to my room during times of need and even to take a break from the norm.

David became very comfortable with coming to me when he needed a talk, help with an assignment, or had a problem. I have taken time outside of school to interact with the student in a mentoring capacity due to the nature of the need and the expressed interest by the parents of the student to form this mentoring relationship.

How has it helped, you ask? Well not only have I been labeled as "uncle" now, but I also receive hugs almost every day. He is sure to come and greet me daily. In addition, his achievement has skyrocketed and the students I currently teach are able to look up to him...another win here for going the extra mile. I could have not taken the time but consider how that may have negatively affected the student (who, I might add, is very intelligent with tremendous potential).

Being an educator is not easy for obvious reasons. Therefore, being a passionate educator who is willing to go the extra mile is not as common as it should be. Consider how things might change for all parties involved if the student(s) felt supported. There is much more to be gained from such an experience than what may be lost. John Holmes states that "there is no better exercise for the heart than reaching down and lifting people up."[2] Go the extra mile. It might just light the fire in a student that can't be extinguished.

Reflection Questions

1. How have you stepped out of your comfort zone in your personal life?
2. How have you stepped out of your comfort zone as an educator?
3. How could you step out of your comfort zone? What are the potential benefits?
4. Think about an individual who may need what you have to offer. Who is that person? How can you "go the extra mile?"

The Power of Your Words

Communication is a social skill that is integral to the existence of any individual. In fact, we are social beings by design. How we communicate is in part determined by our bank of knowledge; in this case, the depth of vocabulary that we have, and how we use it. How we articulate our passions, desires, and dreams is just as important as what they are. There is power in your words. Is the point to use language that is above another's capacity to understand? Absolutely not. However, there is a certain power in the words one chooses to articulate his or her intentions. There is power in what you say. In fact, there is power in saying what someone else has said.

One of the key pieces of my classroom is writing, one form of communication that I practice and dialogue with students about all year. Though sometimes students consider it to be a cumbersome task, it is a necessary life skill to be able to write for a variety of purposes. Expository or nonfiction writing reflects what happened or might explain the rationale, history, or reason(s) for an occurrence. Therefore, it is necessary to learn how to explain and elaborate. In addition, since it is not a narrative form, it often lacks the flair of figurative language, and it is necessary for the writer to develop this form of writing. Using quotes is a great and powerful way to do so.

Dissecting quotes and understanding the meaning behind them aids students in determining whether it might be relevant in writing, and how it can be used to engage the reader and/or listener and solidify the intended message. Consider the quote:

"Words are like paint in which the writer becomes the artist and creates a masterpiece."
 – Dene Gainey

Here, words are being compared to paint, and metaphorically, writing is being compared to artwork. In this way, the writer can now form an explanation to support how this statement applies to his or her writing, furthering the explanation and engaging the audience, prompting them to think as they read. Quotes are powerful, and modeling this for students will enable them to not only notice the power of quotes, but also begin to manipulate words themselves.

Reflection Questions

1. Identify five words that you use most often. What themes exist, if any?
2. Are you intentional with your words? Reflect on a time where your words transformed or were transformative.
3. Reflect on a time when your words did not have the desired impact. How has this experience changed you?

Driven

One who accepts the call of teacher and truly feels it is his or her role in life accepts more than just the act of passing on knowledge; it is more than a 40-hour a week job. It is not just a hobby - it becomes life. It is life and breath of the individual who takes on this task, since teaching is but one of the jobs that teachers really have. From counselor to nurse, from uncle to dad, and from teacher to mentor, a true teacher who cares about the students in his or her direct environment digs deeper, goes further, stretches wider and does what is necessary to meet the clear and present needs of the students in his/her care.

You may ask why this is the case. You may wonder why a true teacher pushes forward despite the many challenges that plague education today. These challenges are on many levels, which include new laws and guidelines that are constantly being thrown at you, and the constant pressure for improving teaching and learning so that students can perform and grow. The truth is that not everything experienced as an educator is positive. In fact, unavoidable things happen — you make mistakes, you reveal your humanity. Despite the potential setbacks, you may ask yourself where the drive comes from that encourages the teacher to persist, against all odds.

The Perception

One of the biggest challenges as an educator has been perception. Perception is a visual representation in the mind. Merriam Webster's definition is, "a mental image."[1] How do you "view" the challenges, limitations, and setbacks experienced as an educator? How do you maintain a student-centered view, regardless of the potential barriers that often attempt to limit your scope of influence? It may be the barrier of persecution or misunderstanding. It may be the pressure of student performance on standardized tests. It may be that thing that desires to take your focus from the very reason you started teaching.

With the student in mind, the diligent and driven educator finds ways to meet required educational objectives as well as student-driven needs. The students are stakeholders, and educators must have this understanding to prepare them for their paths in life. I must say that there have been times for me in which I have questioned why I go to such lengths to be there, in whatever capacity for students. There is a greater synergy within me that compels me to pursue, which requires that my perception is correct.

The Action

What are the actions of an educator that are connected to perception? How does perception lead to action? What actions depict an educator driven by passion? How does the educator embrace issues and challenges? What happens when the plan doesn't work?

If the goal is to foster a student-centered environment where the student is the complete focus, and I mean the whole student, then the decisions made about the classroom should reflect this activity. You have heard the phrase many times I am sure, that actions speak louder than words. Indeed, it is still true. We think; therefore, we act. We are beings of action as educators. We are shaping the next generation; we are the catalysts by which students become leaders. Without the cultivation, leadership, inspiration, motivation, building, and enriching of students, then we cannot see them "C.L.I.M.B.E."

The Will

One of the greatest facets of an individual is the will, or the option to choose what one will do or how one will perceive and act. When you are challenged by administration because you have a totally different perspective or perception of what students need in the classroom, what choice do you make? Do you decide on what YOU as the skilled educator knows is best for the current-year students, or do you act based on administrator pushback? When you have parents that do not agree with your teaching style, do you continue to go down the path that you are driven, or do you side with parents and provide alternatives to satisfy them? When you have fellow educators who are unwilling to grow and change, but would rather stay stuck in yesterday, do you allow yourself to adopt a similar lackadaisical attitude, or do you realize the growing need for innovation and change and act on it? These can often be tough decisions for educators.

The driven educator understands his or her responsibility to be relevant and the duty that educators have to serve the students. With that in mind, the educator doesn't stop learning and growing. He or she shares that learning with both in-school colleagues and with those connections beyond the school campus. As practitioners, we must constantly learn, practice, and evaluate (reflect on) our practice for continued improvement. If the educator ceases to learn, this diminishes the potential impact on students (as well as the educator him/herself).

The Resolve

When the day ends, will the educator be pleased with the strides he or she has made to prepare students to achieve greatness? The student-centered classroom requires a perspective shift, as learning can occur in a variety of ways with a focus on student empowerment to maximize learning experiences. In a student-centered approach to learning, the teacher intentionally acts as a facilitator — offering feedback, guidance, and challenge to students. The result is that students own their learning and become empowered to actively engage, construct, create, define, extend, and challenge both themselves and others. These are simply a few of the active verbs associated with student learning. When students are the ultimate and driving focus, they tend to determine what is taken away from an experience, or even what experiences are necessary. In this way, educators can move away from typical ways of teaching, learning, and assessment to more authentic and meaningful forms.

Reflection Questions

1. Empowerment helps to build confidence. What is one way that you've been empowered? How have you empowered others?
2. We likely all have experiences where we tried and didn't see success. How have you overcome these?

Intentional

I have always been a fan of intentionality. After all, we don't plan to operate by chance or mistake, do we? Well, I believe that in life, we discover purpose, passion, and our niche, and we act on the purpose we discover. It is no coincidence that you are reading these very words because at best, they are a reminder that we have a part to play in this tangled web that we weave. Where would we be without the doctors who so delicately aid us in maintaining our wellness? How far could we go on our own if there were no physical trainers who coached us about endurance? Where would we gain that motivation, spark, and zeal for learning if it weren't for those teachers we had who cared enough to ensure we "got it?"

Suffice it to say that somewhere on this life road, we have either been intentional ourselves, or encountered some intentionality. And thankfully so, right? Consider where you might be if you didn't. I know that I would not be on this path had someone not been intentional about guiding and teaching me. Even more, think of the people in your life now who are intentional in their contributions to your motivation and confidence, and make life meaningful and fun.

Merriam Webster provides the following as a definition for intentional: "done with intention or on purpose."[1] I distinctly recall my childhood, and particularly my father, Daniel E. Gainey, who has transitioned. He was quite intentional in everything that he did. He operated with wisdom like no other and always dealt with his children with exactness and purpose.

I learned a whole lot more about this as an adult than I would have ever considered as a child. As a high school student who took a bus to school due to being part of an advanced program, my father would drive me to the stop every morning and wait with me before heading into work. Before waiting with me at the bus stop however, we went to Dunkin Donuts. He tended to get his black coffee and coffee roll each time, and I would always get orange juice and a glazed donut. I don't think I will ever forget it.

Clearly, my father paid attention to the earliness of the day and wanted me to be able to eat something before leaving for school; at the time, no one would be awake but him and me. More important though was the time I was able to spend with him, sometimes in silence, since I was half-asleep quite often.

Once the bus arrived at the stop, I would get on and watch my dad drive away as he saw that I was securely on the bus. This was the intentionality of the day, every day. My dad cared enough to see me off to school and take time to make sure I wasn't going without having had something in my stomach. My father was quite strict, but it was in times like this that I saw him a bit differently.

Over the course of my life, my decisions were not always in line with my father's thinking. I was yelled at several times as a kid and sometimes as an adult trying to learn his way. One thing I could ALWAYS count on was knowing that my father did not do what he did for decoration. There was purpose in the message that he sent, sometimes multiple times when I just wasn't getting it.

I recall another story that had to do with my very first car. I was a college student at the University of Central Florida in Orlando, and he had been very good about making sure I had a car. At one point in my junior year of undergrad, something went wrong with the car and it would not start. I was unsure of what to do and called him. He tried to talk me through several things to check what could be the issue, since he worked as a mechanic for 25-30 years of his life.

With no success, he made it very clear to me that being his son (and perhaps a college student) he didn't want me to be overcharged by going to a service station. He got in his truck and drove 300 miles from south Florida, where I grew up, to Orlando. He fixed the car, had it back in supreme condition, and drove right back down to south Florida. Mind-blowing, right? I couldn't believe it, but at the same time, I was proud to call this man my father.

Another instance was when I was away at Basic Military Training and technical school for the United States Air Force. I'd wanted to enlist when I was 18. My dad simply said, "no." Of course, as a teenager, I did not understand why, especially since he provided no explanation. He himself was a veteran of the United States Army, and served as a medic during the time of the Vietnam War. He never talked much about it, but I am certain that it was a rough experience.

I waited until I was 26 and already a teacher, and decided to enlist. I thought to myself: *"He can't tell me no now."* So I arranged everything and had my uncle take me to the airport to leave, having him hold on to my car until my dad would come to get it. My father and mother flew to San Antonio, Texas to my graduation at Lackland Air Force Base, proud of me. In fact, I remember the huge grin my father wore on his face the whole time. I remember the baseball game we attended, courtesy of the Air Force. My father shipped my car to me when I transferred to Keesler AFB for technical school. Again, intentionality. He wanted me to be okay. He ensured that all would be well with the delivery.

My dad often said to me that he didn't want me imposing on others and I grew up with the understanding that he wanted me to be able to sustain myself. He cared enough to show me what responsibility was, in preparation for that one day when he was no longer able to help. I would know what to do, or better yet, have enough of him in me to make the right decisions. Have I been perfect? Absolutely not, but one thing is certain, he did nothing without purpose.

My father struck again when I took my 2007 Honda Accord on the road to visit and needed to change my oil. Typically, I'd taken the car to the shop for the oil to be changed, but at this time, I decided that I wanted to do it myself. My dad was a bit weak and dealing with the results of surgery but was mobile for the most part with an aid. I'd asked him if he would come outside and talk me through what I needed to do. Still sharp as a whip and so caring as a father, he did just that, but didn't stop there. Not only did he ask a few times if I was sure I'd done what he instructed me to, he got underneath my car and tightened everything because he wanted to make sure I didn't run into any problems.

I almost cried right there because of the intentional efforts of my father. I didn't want him hurt, but he knew he needed to do that for me, and he did it! I'll never forget that!

Dad spent several days at hospice, and the second visit was particularly more alarming for me than the first. I had come back to Florida to live after having been in Texas for about a year and a half. I was in Orlando when I learned of the news that changed my whole life, as I knew it.

The story goes like this: my younger brother was in the room with my dad, along with my mom and oldest sister. My mom went into the bathroom and my sister went into the hallway to use her phone. My brother knew that my dad was experiencing some numbness, so he asked my dad to render a sign that he could feel the squeezes on his legs and feet. One leg was swollen and my brother knew that would be painful, so he avoided that.

My dad seemed to be trying to look out of the window and my brother asked if he wanted to be turned around. My dad shook his head, "yes."

Always a timely man, my dad had often left us if we were not ready when he expected or told us to be. Frequently he said, "To be early is to on time and to be on time is late." In fact, he had a habit of backing into parking spaces because he coined the phrase, "I don't want to have to worry about what's behind me when it is time to go." You might compare these two instances and see the same metaphor in both.

That day, my brother told him that he would return at 6:00 pm to check on him. Let's remember that my dad is now looking out of the window and it's a sunny day. My brother was late returning to the room. When he did arrive, my father was gone.

He was intentional even about departing this life. Talk about a life of intentionality. When he left, no one was in the actual room with him. My mom was still in the bathroom.

Of course, these are all stories I share, but all of them have a common denominator. My father's actions were intentional in impact, and intentional in the subliminal messages he sent by carrying them out. He was setting an example, by which he intended for us to follow, or at least attempt to. On his last days on this Earth, I learned so much about him that I would have never known. First, I learned that he couldn't be as active because of his physical limitations (although he was certainly not the type to sit still, ever). Secondly, I was able to take care of him a bit. I was one of seven, but my dad knew we were counting on him, and that for us to turn out properly there were strides and efforts that he needed to make.

He knew all about the "Y" in YOU. We never stop this realization. We are constantly transformed by adversity, trial, and triumph but through it all, embrace the "Y" in YOU.

Reflection Questions

1. What is the value of being intentional?
2. In what ways have your actions been intentional, either personally or professionally?

The Y

Would you have ever thought as a teacher, or maybe just as a person who happens to be a teacher, that you would ever experience pain? No way! Not in the education profession. If I were to poll the general population, I wonder what results would show?

Now I'd say that this is not a topic that I enjoy talking about at all, but I've had a revelation. Pain has a purpose. First, pain is necessary for us to identify that there is an issue somewhere, whether physically, mentally, or emotionally, which needs attention.

Second, pain is a reminder of the imperfect creature I am. It says, "Hey Dene, here is a challenge for you. If you overcome, it has the unlimited potential to make you more than you were and improve from yesterday to today."

Pain is just like people; it comes in many different shapes and sizes. It doesn't favor anyone and has the ability to land on us all. So many times, I've wanted the pain to end, but as I continue to exist on this earth, I acknowledge a different perspective of the pain. The pain helped me. The pain reminded me. The pain grounded me. The pain hurt me real "good."

When my father passed away, I didn't know what I was going to do with myself. In my mind, my dad (and mom, who still lives) were the reason I strived and kept going and moving. I emulated them and cared so much about their approval and affirmation. My dad was my strength, and when he left me I felt like Samson (the biblical character), whose strength had been wrongfully taken.

Nevertheless, my dad was ready to get the heck out of here after having raised seven of us to be productive contributors to the society in which we live. He said to give when people take. He said to smile in the face of adversity; he knew of a greater reward for standing strong and that it would come! He stood strong when others decided to sit down. He rescued me in times I knew were impossible. He was in essence the hero who (along with my mother) is the reason I live and breathe air today. Thus, when he took off, I felt like I didn't have that wind beneath my wings anymore.

In retrospect, I wonder if that's why he had to leave - the pain of his departure propelled me into the purpose that he often spoke of in our conversations together. He believed in me when I didn't know to believe in myself, or even what to believe.

Imagine the pain and devastation of a having to say goodbye to a strong father. I had to understand and embrace the pain within this situation. Why? Because there was something to be gained from the pain! If my father were here today, he would say, "I don't know why you're crying; get up and do what is in you to do!"

I gained strength from my dad up until he moved on to a better place. Even during his pain, he was strong! I've fully embraced the conversations I recall having with him — so much so that I passionately pursue them, knowing that he knew *me*! He knew I could, and now I can see it for myself. That's not to say that I still don't have doubts, but the pain reminds me that yes, I can, even when the odds say I can't!

As an educated black male, the pain, the stigma, and the burden that I carry is to bring change to eyes blinded by untruth, injustice, prejudice, and stereotypes that would suggest that I'm not good enough. The realization that people look carefully when I walk into a room because they are unsure of who I am, or to deny me the opportunity to be who I am without first passing judgment on me is painful.

It's a pain that shouldn't be, but even in that, it's a pain that has benefits. Some say I'm "this," but I am "that." The parents of students that have labeled me as illegitimate or unworthy of operating in the capacity in which I do, those who are naysayers who have attacked the very place in which I sit and stand...all of that is painful. It's true. But at the same time, there is a "thank you" somewhere inside of me.

I am more aware now and because of it, I go harder. I work harder. I strive harder, despite those who, for whatever reason, try to diminish my capacity with their thoughts, words, and deeds. It's a pain that I endure because I know that someone may look to me as an example of pure love, genuine care, and concern, and a peacemaker, just like my father.

I don't wanna (yes, I said wanna) be perfect. I want to work on continuing to make myself better. Perfection assumes that I've learned it all, seen it all, done it all, and that there is nothing more to strive for and achieve. I've learned to revel in my imperfection. The pain of the moment may reveal weakness - it may cause you to be embarrassed around others who may be better than you (or perpetuate themselves as such). However, it is an opportunity to identify areas in need of strengthening and work toward making yourself (*myself*) better than you were the day before.

I'll never stop trying to be more and do more at every chance I get. I'm not what I've gone through. Tomorrow isn't promised - so the pain, as hard as it may be to accept at times, is necessary for life and certainly not in vain.

If pain greets you at the front door, know that it has value, and shift your perspective to the place where you can see that value. Use it to be better than you were before. Also, never forget the power of YOU. You are the only you that will ever be. Serve others and be the best version of you!

Reflection Questions

1. Pain is never fully escaped...so, then, how might we use it to power us?
2. What experience(s) have you had, that clearly allowed you to be more "you" than you had been before?

The Power of YOU

To be the best version of who you are
Is a role no one else can play
For the authenticity hidden within
The way you do and the things you say
There is no other quite like it
It is part of our diversity
It helps us to see in different ways
As we work to build community
Why not be the original
They say it has more value anyway
There is so much power when we unify
Many cultures, perspectives, and ways
Ways to do, ways to view & ways to think
Ways to feel, ways to heal & ways to act
A melting pot of the minds
Synthesizing new ways to be exact
There's no telling what could happen
When authenticity comes together as one
For limits are no more, in this case
There's nothing that can't be done!

Dene Gainey, 6/23/2017

Reflection Questions

When They Don't Know Your Name

1. Reflect on an experience you've had, or something you've done, for which you were not given credit. How did it shape you?
2. Identify three traits that describe your character. How did these traits become part of you?

The C.L.I.MB.E. Philosophy

1. What is one thing you can do right now to help your students and/or colleagues to C.L.I.M.B.E?
2. What is your personal or professional philosophy when it comes to growth and development? What perspectives constitute your practice?

REFLECTION QUESTIONS

The Success Initiative

1. How do you define success?
2. Reflect on an experience that you considered successful. What was the biggest obstacle?
3. Is success really success without challenges or obstacles? Why or why not?

We Have the Light

1. What talents, skills, or experiences do you have that could encourage others/your students (if you are an educator)?
2. How would you approach others (your students) if you knew that the power of impact was guaranteed?
3. Why is perseverance so important? How would you (or do you) teach tenacity to students?

Turn the Page

1. What talents, skills, or experiences do you have that could encourage others/your students (if you are an educator)?
2. How would you approach others (your students) if you knew that the power of impact was guaranteed?
3. Why is perseverance so important? How would you (or do you) teach tenacity to students?

When the Call and the Passion Collide

1. What are you being "called" to do?
2. What is the thing that you feel most strongly about (passion)?

REFLECTION QUESTIONS

3. How does passion transform a mindset or a will to do?

Going the Extra Mile

1. How have you stepped out of your comfort zone in your personal life?
2. How have you stepped out of your comfort zone as an educator?
3. How could you step out of your comfort zone? What are the potential benefits?
4. Think about an individual who may need what you have to offer. Who is that person? How can you "go the extra mile?"

The Power of Your Words

1. Identify five words that you use most often. What themes exist, if any?
2. Are you intentional with your words? Reflect on a time where your words transformed or were transformative.
3. Reflect on a time when your words did not have the desired impact. How has this experience changed you?

Driven

1. Empowerment helps to build confidence. What is one way that you've been empowered? How have you empowered others?
2. We likely all have experiences where we tried and didn't see success. How have you overcome these?

REFLECTION QUESTIONS

Intentional

1. What is the value of being intentional?
2. In what ways have your actions been intentional, either personally or professionally?

The Y

1. Pain is never fully escaped...so, then, how might we use it to power us?
2. What experience(s) have you had, that clearly allowed you to be more "you" than you had been before?

About the Author

Dene Gainey is an educator and lifelong learner from Orlando, FL with a Bachelor of Science in Elementary Education (University of Central FL), a Master's of Education in Instructional Technology (American Intercontinental University), and is a current doctoral student. Currently with twelve years of teaching experience, Dene functions in various capacities in the education world to include: English-Language Arts teacher, technology teacher, and gifted teacher & coordinator. He is currently the leader and facilitator of the Battle of the Books club at his work location.

Dene has a passion for the C.L.I.M.B.E., celebrating diversity, building community, project-based and problem-based learning, as well as the student-driven classroom. As an educator, Dene feels it is his niche to build bridges and fill gaps, not to mention, give meaning to learning experiences, and use all his skills and talents to motivate students to be "more." As a veteran of the United States Air Force, a singer and songwriter, actor and author collectively, Dene incorporates various techniques in the classroom to make it inviting for students, innovating teaching and learning.

He recently collaborated in the *EduMatch Snapshot in Education (2016)*, released in December 2016. He also is a contributing author for the *EduMatch Snapshot in Education (2017)* edition, as it is a collection of educators in the trenches writing about topics of great interest to them as practitioners. Possessing a genuine love for writing and sharing, he continues to write via his educator blog (www.denegainey.me), and will continue to write collaboratively, as well as pursuing personal writing projects in the near future. His "one word" that encapsulates his day-to-day role and function in the classroom is "IMPACT."

Other EduMatch Books

EduMatch Snapshot in Education (2016)
In this collaborative project, twenty educators located throughout the United States share educational strategies that have worked well for them, both with students and in their professional practice.

OTHER EDUMATCH BOOKS

The #EduMatch Teacher's Recipe Guide
Editors: Tammy Neil & Sarah Thomas
Dive in as fourteen international educators share their recipes for success, both literally and metaphorically!

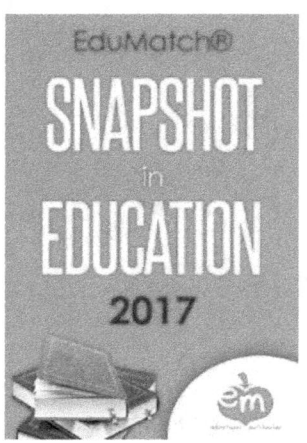

EduMatch Snapshot in Education (2017)
We're back! EduMatch proudly presents Snapshot in Education (2017). In this two-volume collection, 32 educators and one student share their tips for the classroom and professional practice.

OTHER EDUMATCH BOOKS

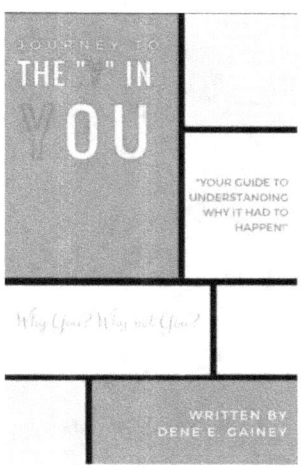

Journey to The "Y" in You by Dene Gainey
This book started as a series of separate writing pieces that were eventually woven together to form a fabric called The Y in You. The question is, "What's the 'why' in you?"

The Teacher's Journey by Brian Costello
Follow the Teacher's Journey with Brian as he weaves together the stories of seven incredible educators. Each step encourages educators at any level to reflect, grow, and connect.

OTHER EDUMATCH BOOKS

The Fire Within
Compiled and edited by Mandy Froehlich
Adversity itself is not what defines us. It is how we react to that adversity and the choices we make that creates who we are and how we will persevere.

EduMagic by Sam Fecich
This book challenges the thought that "teaching" begins only after certification and college graduation. Instead, it describes how students in teacher preparation programs have value to offer their future colleagues, even as they are learning to be teachers!

OTHER EDUMATCH BOOKS

Makers in Schools
Editors: Susan Brown & Barbara Liedahl
The maker mindset sets the stage for the Fourth Industrial Revolution, empowering educators to guide their students.

Divergent EDU by Mandy Froehlich
The concept of being innovative can be made to sound so simple. But what if the development of the innovative thinking isn't the only roadblock?

OTHER EDUMATCH BOOKS

EduMatch Snapshot in Education (2018)
EduMatch® is back for our third annual Snapshot in Education. Dive in as 21 educators share a snapshot of what they learned, what they did, and how they grew in 2018.

Daddy's Favorites by Elissa Joy
Illustrated by Dionne Victoria
Five-year-old Jill wants to be the center of everyone's world. But, her most favorite person in the world, without fail, is her Daddy. But Daddy has to be Daddy, and most times that means he has to be there when everyone needs him, especially when her brother Danny needs him.

OTHER EDUMATCH BOOKS

Level Up Leadership by Brian Kulak
Gaming has captivated its players for generations and cemented itself as a fundamental part of our culture. In order to reach the end of the game, they all need to level up.

DigCit Kids edited by Marialice Curran & Curran Dee
This book is a compilation of stories, starting with our own mother and son story, and shares examples from both parents and educators on how they embed digital citizenship at home and in the classroom.

OTHER EDUMATCH BOOKS

Stories of EduInfluence by Brent Coley
In Stories of EduInfluence, veteran educator Brent Coley shares stories from more than two decades in the classroom and front office, stories illustrating the life-changing power we possess.

The Edupreneur by Dr. Will
The Edupreneur is a 2019 documentary film that takes you on a journey into the successes and challenges of some of the most recognized names in K-12 education consulting.

OTHER EDUMATCH BOOKS

In Other Words by Rachelle Dene Poth

In Other Words is a book full of inspirational and thought-provoking quotes that have pushed the author's thinking, inspired her, and given her strength when she needed it.

To Whom it May Concern
Editors: Sarah-Jane Thomas, PhD & Nicol R. Howard, PhD
In *To Whom it May Concern...*, you will read a collaboration between two Master's in Education classes at two universities on opposite coasts of

OTHER EDUMATCH BOOKS

the United States.

One Drop of Kindness by Jeff Kubiak
This children's book, along with each of you, will change our world as we know it. It only takes *One Drop of Kindness to fill a heart with love.*

Notes

2. The C.L.I.M.B.E. Philosophy

1. Fulmer, S. M., & Frijters, J. C. (2011). Motivation during an Excessively Challenging Reading Task: The Buffering Role of Relative Topic Interest. *Journal of Experimental Education, 79*(2), 185-208.

4. We Have the Light

1. https://www.merriam-webster.com/dictionary/consume

6. When the Call and the Passion Collide

1. (n.d.). call | Definition of call in English by Oxford Dictionaries. Retrieved January 10, 2018, from https://en.oxforddictionaries.com/definition/call
2. (n.d.). passion | Definition of passion in English by Oxford Dictionaries. Retrieved January 10, 2018, from https://en.oxforddictionaries.com/definition/passion

7. Going the Extra Mile

1. (n.d.). Luke 12:48 KJV - But he that knew not, and did commit - Bible Gateway. Retrieved January 10, 2018, from https://www.biblegateway.com/passage/?search=Luke+12%3A48&version=KJV
2. https://www.goodreads.com/quotes/28364-there-is-no-exercise-better-for-the-heart-than-reaching

9. Driven

1. https://www.merriam-webster.com/dictionary/perception

10. Intentional

1. https://www.merriam-webster.com/dictionary/intentional

www.ingramcontent.com/pod-product-compliance
Lightning Source LLC
Chambersburg PA
CBHW071253070526
44583CB00017B/2448